The LIST

INGREDIENTS FOR THE MARRIAGE OF YOUR DREAMS

ROGER D. MILEHAM

The List

by Roger D. Mileham
copyright ©2018 Roger D. Mileham

Trade paperback ISBN: 9781439246337

Cover design by Martijn van Tilborgh

The List is also available on Amazon Kindle, Barnes & Noble Nook and Apple iBooks.

Contents

Dedication

To my wife and best friend, Dawn

Warning: This is not just a book to read because you have nothing better to do. This is a workbook. If you only read this book, it will mess with your head. If you work this book, it will change your life and the life of your spouse. Put the book down and walk away if you don't like a challenge. This book is only for real men and women who want a great marriage.

If you are still reading this, you now have to buy this book because nothing is free. Get out your purse or wallet and buy this book today. It will change your life and the money will change mine. It will be worth it. (No money-back guarantees.) If you work this book you will have a great marriage. If you only read this book, you will understand how to have a great marriage while existing in a mundane one.

Work the book.

Foreword

MARRIAGE: NOW THERE'S AN INSTITUTION that has had some ups and downs. Many people have attempted it and have failed. Some try it three or four times. Hollywood makes an art out of doing it over and over again. So why is it so hard for others and seems so right for only a few. Why do we go through the trouble of all the wedding ceremony and all the debt if we are reluctant to the fact? Is it that we just can't break the tradition? Is it because we have been told that living together is a sin? Is there more to this marriage thing than we really know?

This book was written to possibly make some sense of marriage and also present a way to make it work.

My name is Roger Mileham. I have been married forever, or so it seems at times. My wife would tell you the same. We have actually been married for 35-plus years...a milestone for some. Others have been married twice by then.

In 35 years we have had some great times and some great fights.

I have slept on the couch a few times. Other times I have withheld sex from my wife as a punishment. It doesn't seem to work though. However, it does work in reverse very well. Dawn and I have come to the conclusion that marriage is the closest to heaven or hell on earth you will ever get and you can make it one or the other. We have had both. Heaven is a lot more fun and it costs you less. So how do you create a great marriage? Let's look and see.

The thrill is gone.

Do you remember what it was that first brought you two together? Maybe she was Just looking too good that day or maybe he was just too charming. Something happened that got you two together. Sometimes it's a friend that introduces you to the person that you end up walking down the aisle with. Maybe it was Jack Daniels that got you two together. Either way you are married, hitched, joined together, you've tied the knot or whatever else you want to call it.

Whether you have been married a year or 10 years, I can promise you that there will come a day that you just don't feel thrilled about being married. I mean to the point that the other person could drive your car off a cliff and you would cry because they wrecked your car. You would call the insurance company before you called the ambulance.

There are times that you just don't feel it. You don't feel in love anymore. Then you begin to wonder if you ever really loved the person. You wonder if they ever really loved you. You have kids and that was an awesome experience. (Guys, I'm talking about the birth, not the conception) You have done some great things together but you just don't feel in love anymore. Well, if you were still dating you could just break it off by saying something like "I think we would be better off as friends." But when you're married it is a little more complex than that. So what do you do when you don't feel in love anymore?

Well, because this book is about having a great marriage you don't get to be a pansy and quit. You will have many opportunities and a hundred reasons to quit but anybody can take a mulligan. That won't make the next marriage any better. You don't get to quit. You get to learn how to fall back in love with the person that you once loved.

I have fallen back in love with Dawn about three times in the last 35 years. I believe she has fallen back in love with me at least 10 times. (Some people are harder to love than others).

So what do you do when the thrill is gone? I mean there is not even a fizzle. You start over. Not with another person but with the one you have.

I am going to teach you how to fall back in love with that loser person that you married. They weren't a loser when you married them. They became a loser over time. You probably even helped them become a loser but we are going to turn it around. This book is going to teach you how to change this marriage into something great. You are going to have to work your tail off but it will be worth it.

I hate books that tell you what to do but don't tell you how to do it. I am going to tell you how. If you take the steps, it will change. If you don't, then you just read another book.

Each chapter of this book will teach you how to have a great marriage.

Let's get started changing this marriage.

CHAPTER 1

Drawing *the* Line *and* Starting Over

I T WAS JUST ANOTHER NIGHT FOR ME. I was coming home from work and then going right back out to work. I got the call that someone needed me to come over to their home and help them out of a bad situation. I am a pastor and that is what pastors do. They help people. As I walked out the door, Dawn said the words I will never forget: "Seems like you minister to everyone but me." Those words turned my light on for years to come.

That was the beginning of a brand new day in my marriage. I realized for the first time that we needed to start the relationship all over again. And that we did.

God's love is unconditional; married love is conditional. Let's face it; you married because that person could do something for you that you could not do for yourself. They brought happiness to your life that you couldn't find on your own. They made you feel like no other person could make you feel. What happened to all of that? They stopped working on your dream. Not the one that they knew about but the one you had dreamed up. At first, everything was going along fine and then the first child came, the debt piled up, the late hours at work began, the softball games started and the list that you had in your mind of how the marriage was going to be is gone forever. For some people the dream has turned into a nightmare. So how do you turn it around? How do you make it better?

Let's work the book.

You have to draw a line in the sand and start over. You could get a divorce and start over with someone else but it won't make it any easier. Your dreams will be the same no matter who you stand at the altar with. The dreams and the expectations never change, only the partner changes. If divorce is so great and it's the answer to a marriage gone bad then why do I counsel people who are on their third marriage? A new partner won't make it better; you have to make the marriage itself better.

Drawing a line in the sand is the most elementary thing you can do, but it is also one of the most difficult. Let's work through it together.

How to Draw the Line

1. Write out the hurts.

(Please use actual working lists at back of book.)

Sit down together and write down the ways that you both have hurt each other over the years. This is not a time to be vague with each other. This is a time to be real. Do your best to not hurt each other more as you are doing this. But I want to make sure that both of you know where the hurts have come from and how real they are. As you are writing them down don't rehash them and spend a long period talking about how bad it was or is.

Dawn and I have done this more than once and her lists of hurts are always longer than mine. Because I am a guy, my one hurt is five times hers because my ego was crushed (5 to 1 is the ratio). It is the same as when a man cleans something in the house. We are going to talk about it for a year.

THE LIST OF HURTS

His

1.

2.

3.

4.

5.

Hers

1.

2.

3.

4.

5.

6.

7.

8.

9.

10.

The list for her is longer because in most cases he hurts her twice as many times. If you have to get out more paper, it's okay ladies.

2. Say you're sorry.

Tell each other that you are sorry for the way that you have hurt them. Telling each other that you are sorry is the beginning of something new in your marriage. It's not easy to do but who said marriage was easy? If you can't do this then throw the book in the trash and go watch television, because you are not really serious about having a great marriage.

When you tell each other that you are sorry it has to be more than "sorry." It has to be more than "If (by some miracle of God) I have done anything wrong I want you to know that I am sorry." It has to be something like this. "I am really sorry for the times that I have hurt you". Look at them, make eye contact, and tell them, "I am really sorry for the times I have hurt you".

If you have made it through the first two then you're ready for the really hard one.

3. Make a promise.

Make a promise to each other to never talk about these hurts again. You can never cross back over that line. You can never mention again how you were hurt a year ago or ten years ago. You can only go back to the line that you have just drawn. From here on out it is a brand new day. It's a brand new start.

The fights that you will have in the future (you will have some) will never bring up the past hurts before this date.

There is a remarkable thing that happens to you when you take this step. Over time you forget the hurts. You forget because you don't rehearse them with each other.

You can never build or rebuild anything of real value on a junk heap. You can never build a new marriage while never forgetting or forgiving the past.

4. Mark the date that you started over.

Somehow mark the date that you began this new marriage together and get on with it. Professional sports players do their greatest when they have a new start. Writers have new ideas after taking a break and coming back to the keyboard. Marriages become stronger with every new start. Never look back. Look at what it can become and not what it has been. Dream again.

In 35 years of marriage my wife and I have started over more than once. Each time it was painful but meaningful. We learned to forgive each other and to forget what we had done to each other. We are more in love now than we ever were when we first received the paper that said we were married. Marriage isn't just a piece of paper from the state; it is a commitment to each other and to God who is watching from above to stay together 'til death do us part. It is one of the few lasting commitments that we have left. It's more than a handshake or a signature on a document. It Is two people working together in a world that says commitment isn't necessary; but I think it is and it is the best thing we have going for us.

PERSONAL NOTES FOR CHAPTER 1

CHAPTER 2

For Men Only—Put Your Wife *on* Top *of the* List

FOR MEN ONLY" REALLY ONLY MEANS the women will read this chapter first and as fast as they can.

Men, let me ask you this question: when did the kids take over? I thought I was the first person that she thought of in the morning? Then the kids came along. All of a sudden your offspring are in the bed with you where you used to have fun trying to create them. What happened? If that's not bad enough the dog comes to sleep at the foot of the bed. The love nest, as my wife used to call it, has turned into a daycare center and a vet's office.

Somewhere in this marriage we forgot to keep each other first. The men are no different. We began to work longer hours at our jobs thinking that is what our wife wanted us to do. We need to be the provider of the home and she sure likes the cash but the truth is she would really like for you to spend more time with her. We leave work and go to the gym or to our favorite bar and we forget that we were at one time making our wife the center of our world. How do we get back to the place we once were?

Put them back on top of your list.

It is time that you went back and made your wife the top priority of your life. There is an order to how the marriage is supposed to work. There is a priority list that we should have. Here is how I believe it should look:

1. Your personal relationship with God

2. Your personal "'til death do us part" relationship with your wife

3. Your personal "'til they leave home" (or you have to kick them out) relationship with your kids

4. Your work

If you get any of these out of order it will cost you. I am talking about costing you out of your billfold; real money. Let me explain. If your work is your first priority and your wife is second then when you get a divorce you can work all you want and write her out the check. Do you get the picture?

I am not saying that you need to make her a priority because you don't want to go broke. I am saying that she needs to be a top priority because you made her one when you married her and you need to go back to that.

Let's work the book.

In chapter one we talked about drawing a line and starting over. I assume you have done that and not just read about it. So let's get to work on making this marriage great. I am going to tell you how to make her your first priority and fall back in love with her.

Start by doing the simple things that you used to do for her when she was at the top of your list. Remember when you used to call her at work Just to see how her day was going? Well, now you can e-mail her. Remember how you used to buy her flowers when it wasn't her birthday? You need to do that again.

I don't believe that every guy is the romantic type, but if you are going to have a great marriage, you have to learn some things.

Here is a list of things that you can do to put her back at the top of your list.

1. Buy her flowers—you can get them at Kroger for 12 bucks a dozen.

2. Find a card and sign your name at the bottom. Write "I love you" for goodness sake.

3. Record yourself saying great things about her that she can listen to on the way to work.

4. Plan a date. Don't ask her where she wants to go— plan a date and take her out.

5. Create a DVD of you singing to her (if you can sing) or telling her how wonderful she is (keep your clothes on, please, and the lyrics in front of you.)

6. Buy her something. It doesn't have to be expensive but something that will surprise her.

7. Bathe. No, really, bathe. Women like nice smells.

8. Clip your fingernails and also the toenails that have been digging into her legs.

9. Pick your underwear up from the floor and put them in the hamper.

10. Make out with her like she was your girlfriend.

11. (Make up your own.)_____

12. _____

13. _____

14. _____

15. _____

This list can go on forever. You can think up some things on your own, but you get the point. The remarkable thing that happens as you begin to make her a top priority again is that you fall back in love with her. As we do these things, we believe it will help our wife to fall back in love with us again. But the truth is it causes us to fall back in love. Do you remember when I said that I have fallen back in love with my wife about 3 times in the last 35 years? When you make the choice to begin doing things for your wife then the feelings of love always come back. When you put your wife back on the top of the list and you begin to do the things that you once did for her then all those great feelings for her come full circle. You fall in love all over again. I know that it sounds a little mushy but it's great to feel "in love" with your wife all over again and it is a lot cheaper than a divorce.

Here is another great thing that happens when you put your wife back on the top of your list. She puts you back on the top of hers. You see, if you were doing what you were doing when you first got married then she would run the kids out of the bedroom and put the dog outside. You have fallen into second and third place by default; your fault.

Here comes a real lesson. After about 10 years of marriage I wasn't in love with my wife anymore. She was still very attractive but I didn't feel in love like I did when I first got married. It was the first real time that I wondered if I was going to be able to do this '"til death do us part" thing. I didn't want to feel this way until I died. But I learned a great lesson during this time in my life. It is a lesson that you have to learn if you are going to stay married for a long time. Love is a choice, it is not a feeling. Oh, there may be feelings involved; but it is still a choice. If you choose to show love and to care for someone then the feelings will always follow.

Let me make it even plainer. People love cats. Ugly cats. Cats that won't have anything to do with them. Cats that will not eat their food unless it is the right temperature. Why do they do that? Because they choose to. They love the ugly, ungrateful creature because they choose to. Don't get me wrong; I like pets. Dogs. A pet that will love me back. A pet that will respond to a pat on the head. I like dogs because they will put me at the top of the list.

Back to my point. Love is a choice. You have to choose to love that person all over again and when you begin to do the things that you used to do for them the feelings of love will come back. I promise.

Try it. Begin to show your wife how much you love her and experience the feelings as they come back.

Emotionally Bankrupt

Most women that I meet during a counseling session who are having problems in their marriage are "just done". They have had enough of nothing! They might not have been abused by their husband or been made to do things that they did not want to do but they have not had any deposits made into their heart in a long time. You see, the guy started out making some great deposits in the life of his girl. But after a few years of marriage he forgot that unless you continue to make deposits, then by default, you go bankrupt.

If you could learn anything from this book then learn this one thing; if you make great deposits into a woman that you care about then you will never have to worry about someone making deposits for you. You have to take the time to invest in your greatest asset.

It is amazing to me that men will spend hundreds of dollars to learn how to drive a little white ball into a hole some 500 yards away but won't take the time to learn how to treat their wife. So instead of me bellyaching about trying to get you into some counseling that will cost you money and make you feel like a wimp I am going to do it a different way. For the price of this book I am going to give you some very good advice about women and how to make some real deposits that will keep your woman happy.

Let's work the book.

Women love conversation. You don't have to have all the answers. They just want you to hear how they feel. The greatest deposits you will ever make begin with "Baby, how was your day?" Then sit and listen. Don't say anything; just listen. No- really just listen without turning on the TV. Look into her eyes and listen.

1. Hug her. Without an agenda. Don't hang on her; just hug her. Give a hug instead of getting a hug.

2. Don't make lust to her; make love to her. There is a huge difference. Lust always gets but love always gives. If you are not good in the bedroom it may be that you don't know the difference.

3. Spend time doing some things that she likes. And don't roll your eyes like a four year old while you are doing it. She needs time with you.

4. Be honest. When she asks you which shoe looks the best, pick a shoe. Don't tell her "whatever you like". Pick a shoe and stick to it. Be honest about everything but have some tact. When she asks "do you think this makes me look fat?"—give an honest answer. Answer, "It makes you look a little different than how you really are."

5. Be a man of your word. If you tell her that you are going to do something, do it.

Be her anchor and rock.

The main thing is that you need to make deposits into her life throughout your marriage. She needs to know that even after everyone around her may be using and abusing her you are standing by her. There may be people all around her that are lying to her and are letting her down. But there is one person on this planet that cares about her, listens to her, spends time with her and is a man of his word. That person needs to be you.

PERSONAL NOTES FOR CHAPTER 2

CHAPTER 3

For Women Only—
Maker *of* Men *or* Mice

FOR WOMEN ONLY: THIS MEANS THIS is a chapter the women will read and hope their husbands will read.

Behind, beside, or in front of every good man is a good woman. God told man from the beginning that it was not good for man to be alone. We can't go off by ourselves because we don't know when to come home. Ladies—we need your help. It is not a secret that we can't find anything without you. I can look through the house for a pair of socks for 30 minutes and never find them but if I say the magic words, "Dawn, have you seen my....?" they magically appear.

In the last chapter (which I am sure you have read and read to your husband) I talked to the men about putting you back at the top of their list. In this chapter I want to help you, to help him, have a great marriage.

There are a few things that I have learned over the past few years about myself and about other men that I believe will help you have a great marriage.

Let's work the book.

1. My wife can make me feel like a great man or a small mouse.

2. If she tells me I am great then I only get better. If she tells me that I suck at something then she can do it herself next time.

Men live off admiration. That is why you can tell your man he is fine and he will puff up like a bullfrog. Men love admiration.

Every woman that I have talked with about their marriage will tell me that they just wish their husband would be a man, a man of his word, and get things done. I have only met a few women that wanted a mouse for a husband. You know that type of guy I am talking about. No shoulders and always saying "yes dear, whatever you say." Most women want a real man. They desire a man that will take care of them yet let them be the woman they were called to be. So how do you get your man to be that kind of man? Admiration. Here is a list of admirations for you to give your (mouse) man to get him to be the man he wants to be and you want him to be.

Making a Man

(Please use actual working list at back of book.)

1. You are really good at, (Note: If he is not really good at this don't tell him he is or he will do it from now on. But if you want him to be better at this tell him "You are pretty good at this".)

2. Tell him you believe he can do something.

3. Ask him to show you how to do something.

4. Praise him in public.

5. Let him find out that you are talking great about him to others.

6. (Make up your own)_____

7. _____

8. _____

9. _____

10. _____

Ask him to tell you what he would like to hear from you to make him a better man.

Have you ever seen a man walking down the street with all the confidence in the world? If you haven't seen that lately then go to the nearest gym and you can watch a guy get out of the car with the gym bag in his hand and his gut sucked in as tight as can be. Most men I know want to be masculine. They want to be in charge. They want to be the hero in the movie. They want to save the damsel in distress. I believe God made us that way.

As you read this I don't want you to get the impression that I don't think women can be leaders or that women are not strong but I believe it is the responsibility of a man to take care of his wife. I believe he is responsible for her well being and safety.

Men need to be committed to taking their role as the leader of the family and protector of the wife. The reason that our nation is in the shape it is in today is because men have not filled the role as protector and provider. There are a few women today that want to lead their husbands around by the nose. Most women want to be strong but they want their man to be in the lead. If you want your man to step up to the plate and be a real man you may have to help him out. How? Make him lead.

When God created the woman, her role was to be a helpmate to her husband. She was to help him do whatever he was doing. I tell women all the time that if your husband isn't doing anything then you don't have to help. Make your man lead in all areas of the relationship. If you are both working then you are helping him provide for the family. So if you are helping him in that area then he should be helping with the clothes, cleaning and dinner. You are to help him; not do it all for him. Honestly speaking, if I could come home every day and sit in my leather recliner and get my food on a tray and watch my favorite show I would let Dawn bring it to me. But that is not leading. That is being lazy. But I do know a lot of men who do that every day when they come home. If you are going to get him to lead then you are going to have to make him lead. If he won't lead, don't lead for him.

I know you are thinking that if I don't do it, it will never get done. I am going to help you with that in the next chapter but you have to understand that you are to help him be the leader.

The only thing worse than a man who won't lead is a man who is not allowed to lead. "Mouse men" are what

FOR WOMEN ONLY — MAKER OF MEN OR MICE

I call them. I see them everyday. Not men that may seem a little more feminine than others or a man that may be metro-sexual but a man who has lost his role of leading his wife and family. The wife tells him what to do and when he can do it. Don't make a mouse out of your man.

Let's work the book.

If you don't want a mouse for a husband then stop doing these things.

Making a Mouse

1. Telling him that he is terrible at something.

2. Making fun of him in public.

3. Telling him, instead of asking him, what to do.

4. Making plans for the both of you without asking him. (You sure hate it when he does it.)

5. Talking down to him.

6. Talking negative about him to friends or family.

7. (Ask him to tell you what makes him feel inadequate.) One thing you will discover most about your man is that he never wants to feel disrespected. If you ask a man if he was given the choice to be loved by his wife or respected by his wife, he would choose respect every time. Respect from your wife is the greatest form of love.

The biggest question to ask yourself is, "is your man becoming more of a man or more of a mouse because of you?" Remember whatever you help create is what you will have.

PERSONAL NOTES FOR **CHAPTER 3**

CHAPTER 4

The List — Stop Shooting *in the* Dark

I WAS ON MY WAY HOME FROM work one afternoon and decided to stop by the store for something and while in the store I got a bright idea. I hadn't done anything great for my wife in a while so I thought I would get her a dozen roses. I took great care in picking out the roses that looked the best and that had the best fragrance. I took the time to borrow a pen from the cashier to sign my name on the card with just a small note that said "I love you".

I handed them to my wife, who at that time looked as if she may have had a bad day. To my surprise she simply said thank you and proceeded to tell me that she really doesn't like roses. She prefers plants. I learned a valuable lesson that day; it doesn't do any good to shoot in the dark. If you are not doing what your spouse likes you are just wasting your time and getting your own feelings hurt in the process.

Let's take a look at what you have learned up to this point. You have to draw a line in the sand and start the marriage over. You have to place your wife on the top of your list and wives have to let their husbands lead in the relationship. Remember we are making men, not mice. If you got through the first of this book the rest will become really fun with a lot less work.

Marriage has never been easy but it can be fun. You just have to know what you are doing. It took me years to really understand what my wife wanted. I shot in the dark many times. I found out that a lot of what I was doing Dawn couldn't care less about and some of the things were a big deal to her. I got so frustrated in the early years of our marriage that I made the mistake of saying "well, just tell me what you want and I will do it for you". I took it a step further. Write it down for goodness sake and I will do everything on the list. Just stop making me try to figure out what you want.

That is how this book came about. One afternoon Dawn sat down at the kitchen table and began to write on paper what she really wanted out of our relationship. Not to be outdone; I wrote out my own list. The rest is history. The rest is a great marriage.

She wrote down silly things like please pick your underwear up off the floor and put them in the hamper. Take the garbage to the road on Thursday before the truck comes so that I don't have to take it to the curb.

My list was a little more serious. I wrote things like let's make love twice a week. Let's go deer hunting together. I need you to wash my clothes and make sure that dinner is ready when I get home. You know, serious stuff like that.

All joking aside, we found out some great things about our marriage when we wrote out a list for each other.

The list does exist.

Make no mistake about it; you have a list. You may have never written it down on paper but you have a list. When you got married you had an idea in your head of what you really wanted in the relationship. I am not sure what women want but I do know what Dawn wants because she has written it down for me to see. When I first got married I thought I would have sex with my wife every day. That is almost too funny to type after 35 years. We all go into a marriage with this great list in our heads that needs to be put on paper.

My list is short, shallow and easy.

My list was easy as pie. Sex, food, clothes; in that order. Most men are not really that hard to please. There are a few men that want to think they are deep but if you feed them, put clothes on them and take their clothes off they're pretty much good for another week. We do need to be told that we are good at things with our clothes on and off. We need to feel like the lady we are married to thinks of us as a real man. My list has gotten a little more detailed in the last 35 years but it is short, shallow and easy.

Her list is long, deep, and difficult.

The first time that I wrote out my list you could put it on an index card. I had to go out and buy more computer paper for Dawn to finish her list. It was long and detailed. It was color coated and laminated with bulleted points. Well, maybe I'm exaggerating a bit but her list was a lot different than mine. Women are really complicated but if you have a list to work off of then it gets a lot easier.

The list changed everything.

For years we had been trying to figure each other out but on that day everything was right out in the open. The light had been turned on and now we could see all that we needed to do and all that we weren't doing. The list created some new and exciting challenges for the both of us. So let's take a look at what your list might look like.

How to create the list:

This may seem easy for most people but as you get into it, it is not as easy as you would think. The first thing that you have to do is find a place to be alone. Not with each other but by yourself. A lot of time in the marriage is spent being busy all the time while shooting in the dark. But if you are going to have a great marriage then you are going to have to have some time to plan out this new work.

Spend a few hours working on this. Begin to write out all the things that you really want out of this marriage. I mean write down everything. Don't write down things that are general like "I just want you to love me." Write down things like "I want you to wash your own clothes every day. Mow the grass on Friday. Change the oil in the car every 3,000 miles. Ladies need to write down things that men really understand and men need to write down things that women will understand.

A word of caution to you. Don't ask your spouse what to write. They don't know. That is the reason you are reading this book. If you have to ask your spouse what to write then it is a sign that you have not been thinking for yourself for a long time. Write out what you would like to have in this marriage. This is the only time in this book that I give you permission to be selfish. Write out what you really want out of the marriage.

Let's work the book.

Here is an idea of the first things that we wrote down to get you started.

Roger's List

1. Make love once a week (after 10 years that was safe).

2. Wash the clothes.

3. Clean the house.

4. I will get us dinner every night (we didn't cook much then and she was working full time).

My list was really shallow back then. Basically it was pick up my clothes, wash my clothes, take my clothes off and I will feed myself.

Dawn's List

1. Make love 3 times a week (only kidding.)

2. Help me clean the house.

3. Help me wash the clothes.

4. Pick up dinner before you come home.

5. Take me on a date once a week.

We started really small but this it what it looks like today.

Roger's List

1. Make love once a week (after 35 years).

2. Go on a date once a week.

3. Keep me in the loop about all that Amanda (our daughter) is doing.

4. Work together to clean the house.

5. Work together to wash the clothes.

6. Cook dinner or I will pick something up.

7. Listen to me about what is going on with my work.

8. Tell me that I am great at things that I do.

Dawn's list

1. Take me on a date once a week or every other week.

2. Turn the TV off and have a conversation with me every day.

3. Learn to love our dogs.

4. Take the trash to the road before Thursday morning.

5. Change the oil in the cars every 3,000 miles.

6. Help me clean the house.

7. Help me wash the clothes.

As you can see our list has changed some over the last 15 years. But one of the great things about the list is that once you get the ball rolling, it becomes easier to do and almost automatic.

If you were writing out your list, what would it look like? Would it be a lot different from this? Make sure that your list is realistic. I had one lady tell me that she wanted her husband to have abs. I asked her what if he put on his list that he wanted her to have D cups? She said that would be shallow. She got it. She took the abs off her list. The list can be long or short but make sure that you put together a list that will please you as long as your spouse works the list.

Write out your list.

(Please use actual working list at back of book.)

Husband

The List Name

1. _____

2. _____

3. _____

4. _____

5. _____

6. _____

7. _____

8. _____

9. _____

10. _____

You may not have 10 things on your list. That is okay. Most men don't have a long list of things that will make them happy. And no, you can't put sex on the list more than once.

Write out your list.

(Please use actual working list at back of book.)

Wife

The List Name

1. _____
2. _____
3. _____
4. _____
5. _____
6. _____
7. _____
8. _____
9. _____
10. _____
11. _____
12. _____
13. _____
14. _____
15. _____
16. _____
17. _____
18. _____
19. _____
20. _____

I am just being funny. You may not have 20. If you have 20 then start him out with the top 10. Ten is better than none.

Now the real fun starts.

You wrote out your list and you have checked it twice. Now it is time to sit down together and go over the list. Rules of engagement:

Don't make fun of each other's list.

Gain clarification for each idea.

Ask each other if you can do these things.

Start working the list.

You will find that some of the list will be similar but there will be some surprises. If there is anything on the list that you are sure you cannot do at this time then tell them but let them know that you will work on it. Having children together is a great example.

Out of sight, out of mind.

The next step is to put the list where you both can see it. If you are not looking at it every morning then you will not work it. Dawn and I have ours on the mirror in both bathrooms. Friends come over from time to time and ask us what that list is in the bathroom only to hear me share how it has helped our marriage. I read Dawn's list every morning and make sure that each day I am working the list. She does the same for me.

What the list has taught us.

There have been so many benefits to having the list. The greatest thing that we have learned is that the list causes us to be unselfish. Most people are selfish at heart. We want what we want and we want it now. We have learned that we cannot look at our list to make sure our needs are being met but if we work on each other's list then we create a heart of love for each other. When you begin to do for your spouse what they need, then you find by showing the other person your willingness to meet their needs your heart moves closer to them. If you choose to love someone and do what they need, the feelings will follow. There may be times that you fall out of love with each other emotionally but if you work the list, the feelings will come back.

There is also a great confidence that grows as you work the list. I walk out of the house every day knowing that I am meeting my wife's needs and that she is meeting mine. No one can come between us if we are meeting each others needs. If you are having your needs met at home you don't look for something or someone else to meet your needs.

PERSONAL NOTES FOR CHAPTER 4

CHAPTER 5

Change Your List— Keep Your Spouse

C HANGE, CHANGE, CHANGE; it is everywhere. Everywhere you look the world is changing. Change is good. I like change. Dawn changes her hair color about once a month. I have slept with a blonde, a brunette, a red head, a bald head, (chemo does that) and they have all been the same woman. The only sure thing is that things will change. So it should not come as a surprise to us that marriages do the same thing. They change.

When Dawn and I first got married we sat so close to each other in the restaurant booth that we could not eat our food without getting it on each other. If you were behind us in traffic you would have thought that a two-headed monster was driving the car. Since that time we have learned that we can sit across from each other in the booth and still be in love. We can ride in the car and hold hands without being distant.

As you stay together through the years, the list that you have will continue to change but your partner should be the same. I realize there are many people who are divorced and had to start with someone new; but let's grow with who we have now. Let's look at how the list might change.

Change your list.

In May of 2008, Dawn and I received the call that no one wants to receive. While on vacation the doctor called us to tell us that the lump they found in her breast was cancer. The list that we had on the mirror in the bathroom was about to change in a big way for a long time.

Life has a way of coming and slapping you across the face at times and you have to have a plan, or a list may be a better word. The great thing about moments like this is if you have been working the list for a few years together you have made many deposits in each other's lives. Those deposits help you to carry your spouse's list and yours for a while without going bankrupt.

My wife has made so many deposits into my life. As she began to go through surgery to reconstruct her breast and remove the cancer, months of chemo and days of just not feeling well, it wasn't a hard thing for me to take her list and put mine aside for a while to meet her needs.

I have had the great privilege of doing all that my wife has done for me over the past few years. I never realized just how hard she worked to keep the house going and work a full time job. Doing my list and hers has taught me that I don't ever want to live life without her.

I have found that the longer you work the list, the greater deposits you have put into the life of your spouse. The more deposits you make the greater the interest, I did not realize just how much I loved Dawn until I thought that something could happen to her. It wasn't so much that she may not be here to meet my list but she may not be here for me to meet hers. You really care for others more than you know and the list works more deeply than you could ever understand. Let me explain. Have you ever seen a TV sitcom that had been playing for several seasons? The characters had worked for years and then they come to the last episode and they just barely get through the show without crying and then you find yourself crying? What has happened is they have made deposits into each others lives for years and everything is about to change.

We live in a day and time where things are always changing. We need someone that knows us and will help us when we need it the most. That is really what a marriage is about. We have made it into something shallow and selfish but a real marriage is when you are there to meet your spouse's need no matter what it may be.

There will be times where you will have to sit down together and rewrite the list for what life my throw at you. Remember that the marriage is not to stay the same. It is always changing and it can be for the better if you continue to work the list.

Let's work the book.

About every six months you should sit down together and rewrite the list. If you have situations where your work schedule changes, then the list should change. Let me give you an example. Let's say on the husband's list we have him helping with cleaning the house and on the wife's list she is working fulltime.

Husband

1. wash the clothes

2. cook dinner twice a week

Wife

1. working full time

2. cooking

Well, this seems fair but what happens if the wife is a school teacher and over the summer months she is off work? The list should change to include her doing more of the work around the house. This isn't a hard thing to do but if you don't rewrite the list you will be lost.

I always find it interesting that when I talk with married couples, the woman is doing most of the work at the house and also working a fulltime job. Then the guy always has the complaint that his wife never wants to make love. Here's a thought: maybe she is just too tired and really does have a headache from working all day and doing everything at home as well. Maybe if the husband would help with the home, more might happen in the bedroom.

All I am saying here is that the list will change over the years and that you need to keep it up-to-date.

Write out how or when your list may need to change.

1. _____

2. _____

3. _____

Keep your spouse.

We understand now that there are times that the list will change but we don't have to change partners. The person that you have been with for all these years is the one that knows you the best and has seen you at your best and your worst. They have been through some things with you that have been hard and some things that have been great. You need to keep them. Here's why;

Let's work the book.

1. You have both drawn a line in the sand and started over, right?

2. They now have a list and they are working on it, right?

3. You put her back on top, and you are making him a man, not a mouse.

4. You are no longer shooting in the dark.

5. You understand the list will change.

Write out five more reasons you should keep them.

1.

2.

3.

4.

5.

There will always be some absolutes that will be on your list. They will be the foundation for the relationship but remember that as times change, so do expectations.

As you work together, I hope you begin to see that any marriage can become great again.

CHANGE YOUR LIST — KEEP YOUR SPOUSE

PERSONAL NOTES FOR CHAPTER 5

_____

_____

_____

_____

_____

_____

_____

_____

_____

_____

_____

_____

_____

_____

_____

_____

_____

_____

_____

_____

CHAPTER 6

A Revelation *and* Real Questions

I DON'T CARE WHAT ANY TALK SHOW HOST tells you; divorce is mean. Next to death it is the second hardest thing anyone ever goes through. And make no mistake about it; it is hard on the children. Let me take it a step further; it is hurting our nation. Divorce has created single moms trying to make ends meet. Dads paying child support (if they ever pay) that at any moment could be washed away by the river of debt leaving their kids without support. Divorce creates baggage that people carry to the next relationship and then to the next one.

We have to get back to real marriages that work; to families that are real families; to two people who will not give up just because they don't roll the toilet paper off the right way.

I got married for life. 'Til death do us part. For better or worse. In sickness and in health. Nothing in life is easy. If it is easy; it's not worth anything.

Your marriage is worth the work. It's worth the time and energy it's going to take to fix it. It may be hard to fix but it's not as hard as divorce. In this chapter I want to talk with you about not throwing in the towel. If you are the one on the edge of giving up then I want to talk with you. Don't quit. Don't give up just yet.

If you are married and your spouse still wants it to work, then you can fix it. If your spouse is done, then there is not a whole lot this book or anyone else can do for you. God can help but even He will not break the will of a person. There are a few things that you can do. Go through the first few chapters of this book with your spouse. Create the list. Begin to work it! Decide that you are going to work the list with your spouse. As you do, you will see that your heart will change.

A Revelation

You will not change them. That's right, it is impossible to change your spouse. If you thought "when I get married I will shape them into what I want them to be" you were wrong. Big time wrong. You know that now, don't you? Well, it's a little too late to have that revelation now, isn't it? Not really. There is still hope that the person you walked down the aisle with can be all that you ever dreamed of but you have to know what to do.

It starts with you. That's right, you have to change. Your spouse has given you the list. You know what they want in the marriage. It is on the mirror in the bathroom. You see it everyday. Are you working it? Are you changing yourself to please them? Are you meeting their needs? As you begin to change for them you will see that they will begin to change for you. As you meet their needs they will feel the need to meet your needs.

Here is how it works:

You have to understand that you are not only changing your pattern of behavior for another person, you are also changing your heart and their heart. As you begin to think about meeting your spouse's needs and you begin to work the list, it makes your heart grow fonder for them and messes with their heart in a big way. I am convinced that you cannot be loved by another person who is meeting all of your needs over a period of time and your heart not be changed. If you want to see your spouse change then you are going to have to break through that selfish heart they have by showing them unselfish love for a time.

Here are some questions you may have. Why do I always have to be the one who makes things happen? What if I do all this changing and they just take advantage of me and don't do anything? What if I meet every need they have and they don't do anything, and then what do I do?

Well, let's start with this thought. Up until now you have never had this knowledge to know what to do. You are moving into unchartered waters for you and your spouse. Your spouse is also willing to give it a try so there must be some feelings for you. The real question we should ask is; if I don't do this what do I lose? A marriage that could have been great; a family that stayed together.

Another question to ask, if I do this and it works, what do I NOT have to do? Meet with lawyers. See the kids only on weekends. Pay child support. Be another single mom or dad trying to make ends meet. Lose my stuff. Divide up families and friends. Carry this baggage into the next relationship. Fun stuff like that.

Let's answer some questions:

Why do I have to be the one to always make the marriage work?

Here is the best way to look at this. If it is my fault that things are not going well then that is a good thing. I can't change them but I can change myself. In fact, I would rather change myself then to have my spouse try to do it for me. If I have a list of the changes that I can see then it makes it even easier.

What if I make all these changes and they only take advantage of me? What if they never work my list? Then what do I do?

The list is the real deal. The list tells you where you really are in the relationship. If your spouse has the list in front of them every day and they never even try to work on your list and you are doing their list, then you have bigger issues. Most couples that I have worked with will begin working on the list the first week and then things begin to change. It usually takes one person to get things started but then the other person comes around, if you work the list for three months and you do not see them working the list at all then it is time to sit down together and ask the tough questions. Show them that you have been working on the marriage and ask them to work with you. The real goal here is to make sure that you have done all that you can do to make the marriage great.

What if I am the one who doesn't want to work the list?

Work it anyway. The feelings will come back if you work it long enough. Remember love is a choice; not a feeling. The feelings will follow.

What if we both work the list and are still not happy with each other?

It is not possible. If you honestly tell me that you are living with a person that is meeting all of your needs and you are meeting all of their needs and you both love each other and you are still not happy with each other, then I can't help you. Please don't mistake not being happy in life with not being happy with each other.

How long will it take for the marriage to get better?

How long did it take for you to mess it all up? It will take some time, it will take as much time for you to make this marriage great again as it would take for a lawyer to have all the divorce papers signed, you to have moved out, and the stuff divided up. Great new beginnings take time. You have the time.

Is there ever a need for counseling?

Absolutely. There are always times that you need the advice of other people. That is why you are reading, and I hope, working this book. Make sure you are receiving advice from someone who is in a great marriage. If they have been divorced five times then they are probably not the one to talk with. Here's a good example: if you really want to get physically fit at the gym you don't look for the person with the donut powder around his mouth, sitting in the sauna. You find someone who is working out and looks the way you would like to look. If you have to learn everything from experience then you will kill yourself. Find someone that has been there and can show you how to have a great marriage.

When will the list become obsolete?

There may come a time that you no longer need the list because you know how to meet each other's needs almost automatically. Dawn and I have been doing this for twenty years and it still changes. My wife is always surprising me with new things to do. Me? Well, let's just say I am happy with food, sex, a clean house, washed clothes and sex. Yes, that was on purpose.

Personal Notes for Chapter 6

_____

_____

_____

_____

_____

_____

_____

_____

_____

_____

_____

_____

_____

_____

_____

_____

_____

_____

_____

_____

_____

CHAPTER 7

Singles — Finding *the* List

I SAW HER COME INTO THE RESTAURANT. She had that great style about her. She was dressed in the latest fashion, with her hair shining in the sunlight. Her purse matched perfect with dress and shoes. She would have made any mom or dad proud. Then, in walks her date. His ball cap was bent with a fish hook pinned to it. He wore flip flops and enough grease in his hair to start my car. All I could think was either she doesn't have a list or it's a short one.

In this chapter I want to help those of you who are single, or single again. Maybe someone bought this book and they have begun to do the work in this book and have turned their marriage around and they thought you might like this book. Or maybe you just picked it up for yourself. Either way, I am glad you are reading this. If you are divorced and are looking to do it right this time; welcome aboard.

We can't really talk about the person that you are going to find and spend your whole life with, but we can talk about you.

Finding the List

There is someone out there for you. They are looking for you and you are looking for them. But what exactly are you looking for? What exactly are they looking for?

Is there really someone out there who is a soul mate? Did God create someone just for you? Well, these are all great questions to ask but we really can't answer them all. We can, however, answer the most important one: what are you looking for?

I don't know if you have ever thought about this but you have a list. You have it in your head. You know how you would like them to look and how you want them to act toward you. You know how much money you hope they are making and you hope they like some of the same things that you do. You have just never sat down and written out a list of what you are really looking for. That's about to change.

Let's work the book.

I want you to sit down and begin writing out a list of what you would really like to have in a relationship with someone else. The sky is the limit. It's a dream list, okay?

Write down real things. Here is some help. You probably want them to be attractive. You are going to have to look at them the rest of your life so they need to look nice.

They need to have good hygiene. How much money do you want them to make? You can only live off of love the first month then the bills come due. Do you want them to be a good listener? Do you want them to like sports? You get the idea. Write out a list of what you really want.

Dream list

(Please use actual working list at back of book.)

1. _____
2. _____
3. _____
4. _____
5. _____
6. _____
7. _____
8. _____
9. _____
10. _____
11. _____
12. _____

A dozen is a good place to start. If your list is longer, that's okay but make sure you put down what you really want. Now that you have a list you have an idea of who you should be dating. You want to start dating people that resemble your list.

You are probably not going to find someone who will match your whole list on the first date. You have to get to know people but make sure that you don't date them if they don't have any of the qualities on your list. Another thing to remember is that some things on your list are deal breakers. Let's say you have on your list that one day you would like to have children and the person you are dating tells you they never want to have children. Walk away. That is a deal breaker.

The list is for you to have and for you to follow as you enter or reenter the dating world. Please don't pull out your list on the first date and tell the person your expectations unless you just want to have the rest of the date by yourself. Don't scare the poor boy or girl to death.

Next, keep the list with you at all times. Put it in your purse or wallet as a constant reminder that you are not going to go out with Just anybody. They have to match some of the list.

When you find someone that meets most of the list then you have to determine if you can have a relationship with this person even though they do not meet the full list. Can I live without the other things on the list? Don't think for a minute that you can change them into doing your entire list. That will never happen unless they choose to work on your list. Once you really get to know a person then you can share with them your list. Show them what you are looking for and ask them what they think, but remember that they may not be able to do your list. Make sure you know which things on your list are non-negotiable.

Don't you wish you would have had this list available before that first relationship that went wrong? It's never too late to start over.

THEIR LIST

Now that you have a list, you have created a new challenge for me to issue. What about their list? If you have these high expectations then I would think it is only fair of you to reach a level to catch a guy or girl with such a list.

Let me explain. Let's say you have on your list that you want them to be attractive. Do you go out looking attractive? Let's say you want them to be in great health. Are you in great health? You want them to be neat. Are you a neat person?

If you are going to attract the person on the list that you have made, then you may have some work to do. Remember, you attract who you are, not what you want. With that said, the list that you created is not only what you are looking for but may be what you need to become as well. There may be some things that you need to work on to find a person that meets your list.

Let's work the book.

Find a friend that you can be open and honest with. Show them the list that you have put together. Ask them to be very open and honest with you as you ask them this question: what do I need to change about myself to attract someone that meets my list?

Now write out the list.

(Please use actual working list at back of book.)

1. _____

2. _____

3. _____

4. _____

5. _____

6. _____

You should not have to change everything about your-self to attract this person but don't lower your expectations either. Rise to the occasion. There will be some that would say you should not have to change anything about yourself but we do it every day in the workplace. If you want a better job you become more educated. If you want the list you have created, you may have some changing to do.

Once you have a list of what you are looking for and have made the necessary changes to attract that person, the next thing to do is find them. If your list doesn't include a drinker then stop going to the bar to find them. If it doesn't include children, stop going to the ball-field. Shop at the store which has the things on your list.

A few more dos and don'ts.

Never go on a blind date. They may be blind but you're not. I know you have attractive on your list, right? See them before you date them.

Don't compromise your list for a friend or parents. They don't have to live with the person, you do.

Date them long enough to see if they can continue to work your list. Most people can't fake it over three months.

As the relationship grows more serious, make them put together a list for you. Make sure you can meet their expectations.

I know that most of this may sound simple but most people I have counseled with have never done anything like this while dating. It is important to know what you want and to make sure that the person you are dating knows it as well. Now, with list in hand, go shopping.

PERSONAL NOTES FOR CHAPTER 7

CHAPTER 8

It Takes Three — *for* Those Who Want It All

HAVE YOU EVER BEEN IN THE PLACE in your relationship where no matter what you did you just could not make the other person happy? It was like there was something missing in their life and they were looking to you to fill it. Maybe you are the one that is receiving great things from your spouse but you are still not happy.

Time and time again I have met couples with this issue. They seem to be happy with each other but not really happy with life in general. They seem to have something missing in their life and can't seem to find it. They try new things, and some try a new person, which only creates a bigger mess.

I believe I have an answer to this dilemma. It takes three. After reading and working this book I hope you have found some answers to how to have a great marriage. But that is not all you need in order to live a great life. I don't want to come off to you as being some religious person even though I am a pastor. Religious people scare me.

However, I do believe that marriage was God's idea. He said that it was not good for man to be alone so he created a woman. Thank God for that. God established marriage. SO, if God is the one who created marriage and we are working the list with our spouse then why are we still not content? Why do we still not seem fulfilled? The answer: God.

If you believe in God, and I do, then you have to understand that in all of us we have the desire to know and have a relationship with the

One who created us. God created us that way. We are not complete with just another person. We have to know God.

I believe that in each and every one of us there is a void in our heart that only God can fill. The reason you are having such a hard time meeting all the needs of your spouse is because some of the needs they have can only be met by God Himself.

You may be reading this and thinking, "I don't even believe in God" but the fact is you still have a void in your life that only God can fill. Many have tried to fill this void with relationship after relationship, drug after drug, drink after drink and every time they come up short. I am not saying that you can't have a good relationship with your spouse, but I am saying that you can have a great one with you, your spouse and God.

God is the one that can give you insight on how to have a great relationship with your spouse. Remember He is the one who created them so He knows what will make them happy. You also have to understand that this life will throw things at you where your spouse will not be able to be of much help. We need God in those times.

Let's work the book.

The principles in this book work much the same with God who created us. It is God's desire that we first draw a line in the sand and start our life over. If we ask God to forgive us and to come into our life and give us a brand new start, he will draw the line for us. He will forgive us for the wrong decisions we have made and He will not bring them back up to us later. Then we begin a relationship with Him and make out a list of all the things we would like for God to do for us.

Write out a list of the things you would like God to do for you.

(Please use actual working list at back of book.)

1. _____

2. _____

3. _____

4. _____

5. _____

6. _____

7. _____

8. _____

9. _____

10. _____

It is God's desire to give you the desires of your heart. If God would send his own son to die on a cross for your mistakes He doesn't have any problem answering that list you have just written. But there is another part to this relationship. God has a purpose and a plan for your life.

Now comes the relationship part. Write out a list of all the things you believe God wants you to be. You may not even know where to start so let me be of some help to you.

(Please use actual working list at back of book.)

1. He wants you to draw a line in the sand and start over. Ask God to forgive you of all your past.

2. Believe that Jesus came to earth and died for your sins so that you can be forgiven.

3. Begin reading his word and praying to him about your list.

4. Find a church where they teach the truth of God's word and attend regularly.

5. _____

6. _____

7. _____

You are not here by accident. God has you here for a purpose and a reason. God has even given you your spouse for a reason. The three of you together can tackle anything that life throws at you. We need each other and we also need God.

For the last 35 years I have had a wonderful relationship with Dawn but there has been more than one time that I have had to ask her to forgive me. There have also been times we have had to ask God to help us to forgive each other for things that we have done or said to each other. God is the one who helps us to forgive each other and to continue to work on the relationship.

I know there are many people who have attended church who are now divorced. In fact, the divorce rate in the church is as great as those who don't attend church. But I am not talking about people who simply go to church but about people who will go to God for help. If two people love each other and ask God to help them, he can turn the marriage around and make it great. Give God a chance to change your life.

PERSONAL NOTES FOR CHAPTER 8

CHAPTER 9

SEX—*A* Real Talk

I WAS FINISHED WITH THIS BOOK. I had written all that I wanted to say to help people have a great marriage. Then, I let some of my friends begin to read the material and they told me you can't have a book about how to have a great marriage without talking about sex. So here we go.

I have a list. Guess what number one is on my list. You guessed it. Sex. Guess what number one is on Dawn's list. No, it's not sex, it's conversation. So we talk about sex. Not really.

Sex is good when it is good and even when it is not really good it is still good. That's a guy's perspective. Not just mine, any guy. Any guy that says he doesn't like sex is lying, or maybe lying with someone else.

God created sex. That's what I said, God created it. God also created music. The world has perverted both of those but in the original form in which they were created, they are great. So if God created it, then I believe He wants it to be great in your marriage.

Sex has a very important role in the marriage relationship. Some would have us believe that God created it just for us to produce offspring but God is more creative than that.

Some people even freak out if you use God and sex in the same sentence but you just read one and you didn't die, so let's talk about it.

HOW TO HAVE A GREAT SEX LIFE:
Know the difference between lust and love.

If you are going to have a great sex life you have to know the difference between lust and love. The word lust is a *getting* word and the word love is a *giving* word. Sex was created by God for two people to give themselves to each other, not to get something from each other. There is a huge difference between making lust and making love. If you really want to have a great sex life you have to learn how to show your spouse that you love them during sex. You have to be the person who wants to give to your spouse and not just the person who wants to receive. That means different things to different people, but make sure you are showing them you love them, not Just having your way with them.

FOR MEN:

Romance, Romance, Romance!

Warning: What you are about to read is from a guy's perspective.

All great sex begins with romance. Sex does not begin in the bedroom at night; it begins at the start of a new day when you have the whole day to spark the romance all over again. Most men that I have talked with know a little about sex and know nothing about romance. In fact, most men I have talked with who have had problems in the bedroom know nothing about romance. They are as romantic as a rock. We can fix that.

Here is the formula for a great sex life. Romance + Romance + Romance = Sex

It's that simple. Men who are romantic are having sex, men who aren't, aren't.

When is the last time you have been romantic to your wife. 19_ _? Let's talk to the men about how to be romantic. Do you know what your wife considers to be romantic? Have you ever asked her? Ask her. Is it cards? Flowers? Diamonds? What is it?

Let's work the book.

Have her write out a list of what she thinks is romantic to her. Remember we are not going to spend the rest of our lives shooting in the dark. (Please use actual working list at back of book.)

1. _____

2. _____

3. _____

4. _____

5. _____

6. _____

7. _____

8. _____

9. _____

10. _____

Here are some helpful hints.

1. Cards for no special holiday

2. A planned date

3. A day at the spa without you or the kids (She will come home.)

4. A CD placed in her car of how wonderful you think she is (in the player when she starts the car)

5. Make dinner for her. (candles, yes, candles)

6. A bubble bath ready when she gets home (without you in it)

7. A concert

8. Victoria Secret gift card (no, don't pick something out yourself)

9. Gifts

You get the idea. Get creative about being romantic.

If you are going to have a great sex life you have to have a great romantic life.

So, I assume that your wife has written down for you the things that she believes is romantic so now it is time for you to get to work. Please don't expect her to want to go to the bedroom just because you did one romantic thing today or the next day. These things take time and remember you are not Just being romantic to get her to have sex with you. If that is what you are doing then go back and read the love, not lust paragraph again.

Now that you have a list of what she thinks is romantic then you have to have another list. This list is all the things that she likes as it pertains to being intimate together.

This is a list of all the things she likes and that she hasn't liked for years but was afraid to tell you. Ask her to write out this list. This is not a list that you are to share with your buddies or your closest friends. This is a list between you and the wife that God has given you. This list is as private as your times together are. (Please use actual working list at back of book.)

1. _____

2. _____

3. _____

4. _____

5. _____

The reason I only gave you five places for your wife to write what she likes and doesn't like is because it is not as complicated as we men make it out to be. Women like certain things with their spouse and other things stop the intimacy all together. Ex: bad breath is a killer in the bedroom. Razorblade toenails don't seem to be a turn-on either. The other reason the list is so short is you don't want to have to be thinking about 20 things that you should and should not be doing when you are together.

Time

It does not take time to make lust but it does take time to make love. You need time to be intimate together. I promise you that you will never find the time to be alone together, so you have to create the time. You make time to go to work. You make time to go to church or to play golf, so make the time to be intimate with each other. I know someone is thinking, I like to be spontaneous and creative with my spouse but my response to that is put down the remote control and re-enter the real world with the rest of us.

If you are going to have a great sex life then you have to carve out time for it.

Woman

It is more difficult for me to write to women about how to have a great sex life with my wife looking over my shoulder with a frying pan in her hand but we will give it a try. (I don't believe she is about to cook anything.) Plain and simple, sex is to men what … oh I can't think of anything. Sex to your man is great. We like it.

For some men being intimate with their wife is the greatest feeling of love they have ever experienced. For others it is the feeling of conquest. Still for other men, it is just a great feeling to know that someone thought enough of them to be intimate with them.

Either way you look at it men like to be intimate with their wife. And they don't have to have a reason to want to be intimate. The sun shining is a good reason and the rainy days are a good reason, too.

So what do I need to say to women who are reading this part of the book on how to have a great sex life? I could tell you to have him write out a list of all the things he likes but really now, is that necessary? I am sure he has told you what he likes about one thousand times (today). The only really good advice I have for you is help us to be romantic. Help us to understand what you need to be intimate and then be intimate with us. Here are a few suggestions that 1 believe will help you:

1. Never tell your husband you will be intimate with him on a given day and not follow through. That's like him telling the kids he it going to take them to Disneyworld and then going golfing instead. That's how it really feels.

2. Never wear V. S. to bed and say "let's just cuddle". That's just wrong.

3. Walk him through your list.

4. Never use sex to get your way (that's lust, not love).

5. Tell him what was good and tell him later what could have been better.

What is okay and what is not okay?

What isn't okay...

As a pastor, I have been asked what is okay in the bedroom and what is wrong. The bible says that the marriage bed is undefiled. My advice to any married couple is that if you both are comfortable with what you are doing and if it is done in love then I believe it is fine. There are a few things that i believe are definitely harmful to any marriage.

Pornography

This vice does away with taking the time to be intimate together and offers instant gratification and promotes lust and not love for your spouse. Regardless of what experts say this can kill a marriage. As a teenager, I grew up looking at pornography and had to learn to honor my wife with love and not lust. I had to learn that my wife was more than just a body to gratify my desires and learn to meet her needs. Every man that I have spoken with has to deal with this on a daily basis; even those who love their wife with all their hearts. Don't let it hurt your marriage.

Abstinence for long periods of time

Even the bible says to separate yourselves for a time of fasting and prayer but to come back together so that you are not tempted to commit adultery. You have to make time to be intimate.

Making your private moments public

What you do in private between the two of you needs to stay between the two of you. Don't ruin what you have with them by telling others no matter how wonderful it was.

What happens in _____ stays in _____.
                    your address   your address

What is okay...

It is okay to be intimate with each other at the level that you are both comfortable. If what you do together can be done in love for each other then I believe it is fine. The only thing I will say in this matter is if you can both enjoy each other the way God has created it to be then I believe you can have a great sex life together. People have asked me about sexual aids and items you can buy to enhance your sex life. Even though i don't believe all of these are wrong I do believe that you have to be careful not to take away the intimacy that you have together or to create an expectation that your spouse cannot meet. Just because everyone else is doing it does not make it right. You have to know what is right for you and your spouse.

I do believe the greatest enhancement to your love life is knowledge. The more you know what makes your spouse feel loved, the greater love life you will have. There are also some great books out there that can help you, but make sure you choose those that don't border on porn. Remember you are learning to love your spouse, not lust after them.

It's okay...

...to enjoy your sex life. Our society has made it so dirty and evil that many good people have a false guilt for enjoying their sex life. Remember that if God created it then he created it for you to enjoy it.

It's okay...

...to feel sexually attracted to your spouse. It's not okay to go out trying to feel that way with other people. Save that for your spouse.

It's okay...

...to have a great sex life with the person that God has given to you in marriage. God is the one that said "it is not good for man to be alone" so enjoy each other's company. Enjoy each other's friendship and also enjoy each other's intimate times together.

PERSONAL NOTES FOR CHAPTER 9

The Last Word

I HOPE THAT YOU HAVE FOUND this workbook to be helpful in your goal to have a great marriage. It is just a guide that will get you moving in the right direction. You have a lot of work ahead of you but I believe it will be worth it. The information that you now have from this book will help you to see what a great marriage can be, but it will also open your eyes to how messed up it has become. Don't get discouraged about where you may be today. Be encouraged about where you will be a month or two down the road. It will change. It will get better. Keep working at it. You have a lifetime. My prayer is that this book has helped you. Please let me know.

Acknowledgements

FOLLOWING ARE THE PEOPLE who have helped make this project possible, and taught me that anything is possible with enough friends to encourage you and to deliver a kick in the butt when you need it.

To Dawn, my wife, who has always believed in me and has made our marriage great. Thank you for the first list and for fulfilling mine.

To my daughter, Amanda and my son, Dylan who are the greatest children anyone could hope to have. Thanks for making me laugh all these years.

To Rachel Marler, Starla Skelton and Leslie Nelson who proofread this over and over again. Thanks for teaching me that cat doesn't start with a "K".

To my sister, Robin, who will do anything for me. You are the backbone of a lot of what I do. Thanks.

To Dr. Samuel Chand and his wife, Dr. Brenda Chand—Thanks for believing in me even before I believed in myself. Thanks for the pushes, pulls and shoves to do great things.

To my Dad—Thanks for being the strongest man I know, and proving to me and the world there are still some real men who love their wives all the way to "til death do us part".

To every family of Trinity Family Worship Center, past or present, you guys are a great blessing to me; and to my Elder board who believes in me. You guys are the greatest!

And to my mom, Eva, who never read a book on marriage but was a great wife by following the word of God and praying her husband and children into the things of God. I really miss you. Hope God lets you read this.

And to my grandson Evan who has made my life complete.

About the Author

ROGER MILEHAM is the lead pastor of Trinity Family Worship Center in Hampton, Georgia, and a certified Life Coach through Dream Releaser Coaching. His passion is to help families become whole through pastoring, coaching and conferences. He is happily married to his wife Dawn, and they have two children, Amanda and Dylan and a grandson Evan. Roger is passionate about reaching the next generation with the truth and helping families stay strong in these difficult times. His transparency in this book and in his message has helped others relate and receive hope that their lives and marriage can be changed.

CHAPTER 1

DRAWING THE LINE AND STARTING OVER

The List of Hurts: His

1. _____

2. _____

3. _____

4. _____

5. _____

6. _____

7. _____

8. _____

9. _____

10. _____

CHAPTER I

DRAWING THE LINE AND STARTING OVER

The List of Hurts: Hers

1. _____

2. _____

3. _____

4. _____

5. _____

6. _____

7. _____

8. _____

9. _____

10. _____

CHAPTER 2

FOR MEN ONLY - PUT YOUR WIFE ON TOP OF THE LIST

1. _____

2. _____

3. _____

4. _____

5. _____

6. _____

7. _____

8. _____

9. _____

10. _____

CHAPTER 3

FOR WOMEN ONLY—MAKER OF MEN OR MICE

Make a Man

1. _____

2. _____

3. _____

4. _____

5. _____

6. _____

7. _____

8. _____

9. _____

10. _____

CHAPTER 4

THE LIST—STOP SHOOTING IN THE DARK

His List

1. _____

2. _____

3. _____

4. _____

5. _____

6. _____

7. _____

8. _____

9. _____

10. _____

CHAPTER 4

THE LIST — STOP SHOOTING IN THE DARK

Her List

1. _____

2. _____

3. _____

4. _____

5. _____

6. _____

7. _____

8. _____

9. _____

10. _____

CHAPTER 5

CHANGE YOUR LIST - KEEP YOUR SPOUSE

Updates to His List

1. _____

2. _____

3. _____

4. _____

5. _____

6. _____

7. _____

8. _____

9. _____

10. _____

CHAPTER 5

CHANGE YOUR LIST - KEEP YOUR SPOUSE

Updates to Her List

1. _____

2. _____

3. _____

4. _____

5. _____

6. _____

7. _____

8. _____

9. _____

10. _____

CHAPTER 7
THE DREAM LIST

1. _____

2. _____

3. _____

4. _____

5. _____

6. _____

7. _____

8. _____

9. _____

10. _____

CHAPTER 7

Singles—Finding the List

Changes You Should Make to Attract:

1. _____

2. _____

3. _____

4. _____

5. _____

6. _____

7. _____

8. _____

9. _____

10. _____

CHAPTER 8

IT TAKES THREE—FOR THOSE WHO WANT IT ALL

What God Can Do For You:

1. _____

2. _____

3. _____

4. _____

5. _____

6. _____

7. _____

8. _____

9. _____

10. _____

CHAPTER 8

IT TAKES THREE — FOR THOSE WHO WANT IT ALL

What God Wants You To Be:

1. _____

2. _____

3. _____

4. _____

5. _____

6. _____

7. _____

8. _____

9. _____

10. _____

CHAPTER 9
SEX—A REAL TALK

What's Romantic To Her:

1. _____

2. _____

3. _____

4. _____

5. _____

6. _____

7. _____

8. _____

9. _____

10. _____

CHAPTER 9
SEX—A REAL TALK

The Intimate List:

1. _____

2. _____

3. _____

4. _____

5. _____

6. _____

7. _____

8. _____

9. _____

10. _____

CPSIA information can be obtained
at www.ICGtesting.com
Printed in the USA
FFHW020939240120
58028582-63156FF